Long before the boy band singers of today that stir up young girls' dreams of romance, and long before the Beatles and their near-hysterical fans, there was a young gangly singer with the Tommy Dorsey band who created such an impact on the music world (not to mention his effect on young girls) that the fall-out still resonates today.

His influence on the bobby-soxers was a phenomenon never seen before. The girls would swoon over his music, causing near riots when he appeared in public. They screamed, "Frankie! Frankie!" and his name became a household word.

Francis Albert Sinatra was the unlikely sexual stimulant to the pubescent girls of the time. The way he phrased his songs and the longing he created with his voice seemed to touch their hearts, and they responded with emotional fervor.

By the time he left Dorsey and began singing on his own, opening at the Paramount Theatre in New York, there was no stopping him. The crowds of girls in front of the theatre were so large they filled the street, stopping traffic so completely that the police were called out on a daily basis.

At one point the city had to field 200 men in blue to control the crowds. He was the toast of the music world. His records sold in the millions, and he was still in his 20s.

From Here to Eternity

1953

I remember one of my friends saying I had to see her daughter's room, and when we went in, I was amazed to see that the walls and even the ceiling were covered from top to bottom with photographs of Frankie. It was an incredible era.

But as time passed, something went very wrong with his dream life. His wife divorced him after his various flutters with the Hollywood ladies, including the gorgeous Ava Gardner. He was quick to throw a punch, and the press who once loved him now gleefully recorded his every misadventure. With his record sales plummeting, his record company dropped him. He lost his TV show, and MGM cancelled his film contract… and down and down his career seemed to go.

By 1953, when he learned that Columbia Studios were going to film *From Here To Eternity*, it is said that he asked all his friends to badger Harry Cohn, the studio head, to let him play Maggio. Every other role had already been cast, and the film was about to roll, except for the part of Private Maggio.

Eventually director Fred Zinnemann gave him a screen test, and it was so moving that when Zinnemann showed it to Cohn, he was finally persuaded. Frank would work for little more than the actor's scale, but he got the part.

His gamble paid off: the film was a blockbuster at the box office and a critical success, winning eight Oscars, including one for Frank.

When I came on the set of *From Here to Eternity* for *Collier's* magazine, Frank was hungry for good press. All the stories I had heard about his hatred for photographers made me cautious when I first met him. But he was so agreeable and charming, it was hard to believe this could be the same person.

We went outside on the studio lot and had a Coke together, and I felt it was my lucky day. As it turned out, it was, for I never saw Frank quite as cooperative again. He was professional always, but easy... well, that's another story.

Here was a Sinatra charming and funny, wearing his hat sideways on his head for the camera, pretending to rehearse his lines as he walked on the Columbia Studios lot, and giving me that romantic little-boy-lost look so beloved by a generation of fans. I felt my photographic guardian angel was watching over me that day for sure.

Director Fred Zinnemann comes over to the table with Montgomery Clift and Frank Sinatra, to give them directions for the coming scene.

Frank said he could have been Maggio. He knew this person, he became this person, and his performance was so real that it amazed even his worst detractors and won the hearts of the film critics.

By the end of this film he had regained his old self-confidence, and when he walked off the Columbia Studios lot, he would never look back to his previous bleak times.

Frank enjoyed a laugh on the set with Burt Lancaster, Mickey Shaughnessy and Ernest Borgnine. One day I noticed Frank listening to advice from Burt Lancaster. Burt discussed (or more accurately, powered his ideas across) with Frank about how to play the coming scene.

I've been told, however, that Frank gave his greatest accolade to Montgomery Clift, for his help in defining his role. Deborah Holder, in her book *Completely Frank*, quotes him as saying, "I learned more from him (about) acting than I ever knew before."

↓ Burt Lancaster was dynamic both as an actor and in person. He had an amazing persona, and in all of his scenes, the energy was palpable.

Seen here as Sergeant Warden, he steps in to defend Private Maggio from the threats of the vicious stockade sergeant, played by Ernest Borgnine: his dynamic force is clear to see.

A poignant anti-war film, *From Here to Eternity* was awarded an Oscar for best film in 1953. Burt won best actor, Zinnemann best director, and it won five other Oscars, including Frank's for best performance.

That coincided with Frank's first new recordings with the young composer and arranger Nelson Riddle at Capitol Records. They meshed like Audrey Hepburn in Givenchy.

Riddle's arrangements were made for Frank: to this day they still amaze, and Frank knew then that he was back in a position to call the shots.

The next time I saw Frank was on the set of *Suddenly* in 1954. My agent had asked me to shoot some candids on the film. When I arrived at the studio I found a now totally indifferent Sinatra. It seemed to me at the time that he went out of his way to make it difficult for me to work.

I don't give up easily on difficult assignments – in fact, Frank told me years later that if nothing else I was "persistent". In this case I could see where his head was, and I just packed up the cameras and left.

The Man with the Golden Arm

1955

← Frank getting a feel of the new world he would inhabit for the coming weeks. RKO Studios, Hollywood, 1955.

↓ Before filming began, Otto took Frank around to show him the remarkable set that was being built for the film.

→ → The first reading of the script by all the actors. Preminger listens in the foreground with (left to right) Eleanor Parker, Robert Strauss, Doro Merande, John Conte, Darren McGavin, Arnold Stang, Kim Novak and Frank Sinatra. RKO Studios, Hollywood, 1955.

Fate, however, would bring the two of us together again.

In that same year, my various magazine assignments had caught the eye of the film studios, and they started hiring me to get space in the magazines for their films.

It all started with Warner Brothers' A Star Is Born. This was a major change of policy, as I was a non-union member, and the studios had to pay a stand-by fee for every day I was working on their film.

Then Otto Preminger asked me to work on Carmen Jones and the two of us seem to hit it off well. Amazingly (given his reputation), Otto never interfered with my work. He seemed to feel I knew what I was doing, and gave me free reign.

We were to work together three more times, next on The Man with the Golden Arm, a downbeat story about a drug-ridden drummer written by Nelson Algren. Preminger liked to do controversial films (by the standards of the time), and Sinatra was to play the lead.

Rehearsals begin. Sinatra as Frankie Machine, and Eleanor Parker as his wheelchair-bound wife Zosch, read from their scripts on the first day on set of The Man with the Golden Arm. Director Otto Preminger is on the right.

It was interesting to see Frank, seemingly tentative in rehearsals or when studying the script by himself, become suddenly confident when he stepped into the role. It was if someone else had taken over, and he became that character.

His concentration was amazing. Since I had become one of the crew, I basically became invisible to him, so I was able to document him as he grew into the part of Frankie Machine.

Preminger takes Kim Novak and Frank into his dressing room to rehearse away from the crew. Kim plays a bar girl that Frankie meets after his wife is killed. She fights with him to go cold turkey, helping to get him off his drug addiction. It was a difficult role for Kim.

Otto needed to have a lot of patience with her. While she was a very sweet and attractive young lady, getting her to give a dramatic performance was something else. The extraordinary concentration on Frank's face is apparent as Otto discusses the scene.

Sinatra had to learn to play the drums for his role. Whenever there was a quiet moment on set, he would slip over and quietly practice to himself. Preminger hired the great jazz drummer Shelly Manne to help Frank feel at ease on the drums.

← ← Preminger cues the camera move for a scene in which Frankie Machine tries out for a place in an orchestra, but is too strung out on drugs to make it. Shorty Rogers is top left, in the striped shirt, and composer Elmer Bernstein (who was nominated for the film score by the Academy) leans on the piano while Lou Levy is playing.

↓ Frankie Machine tries and fails at the audition, so strung out he cannot find his way. Seated behind Frankie is the great jazz drummer Shelly Manne.

→ Frank lies alone with his drums on the dimly lit RKO set, I'm sure trying to get into the head of the character he is playing: no longer able to work, needing a fix to keep going, Frankie Machine knows that sooner or later he'll have to find his old drug dealer, and then he'll be right back in the trap that sent him to jail.

Otto Preminger watches Frank Sinatra and Kim Novak rehearse. On his left is cinematographer Sam Leavitt, and in the center is sound engineer Jack Solomon.

Frankie can no longer make it without a fix. He calls his old dealer Louie (Darren McGavin) who comes to the apartment. When Frankie's wife learns he is back on drugs, she calls Louie, who comes back when Frankie has left. They fight, and Zosch is pushed over the balcony to her death.

Otto demonstrates how he wants Eleanor Parker to lie, and watches as Frank and Eleanor rehearse the scene

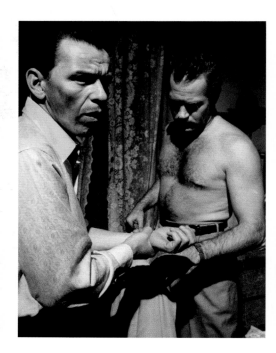

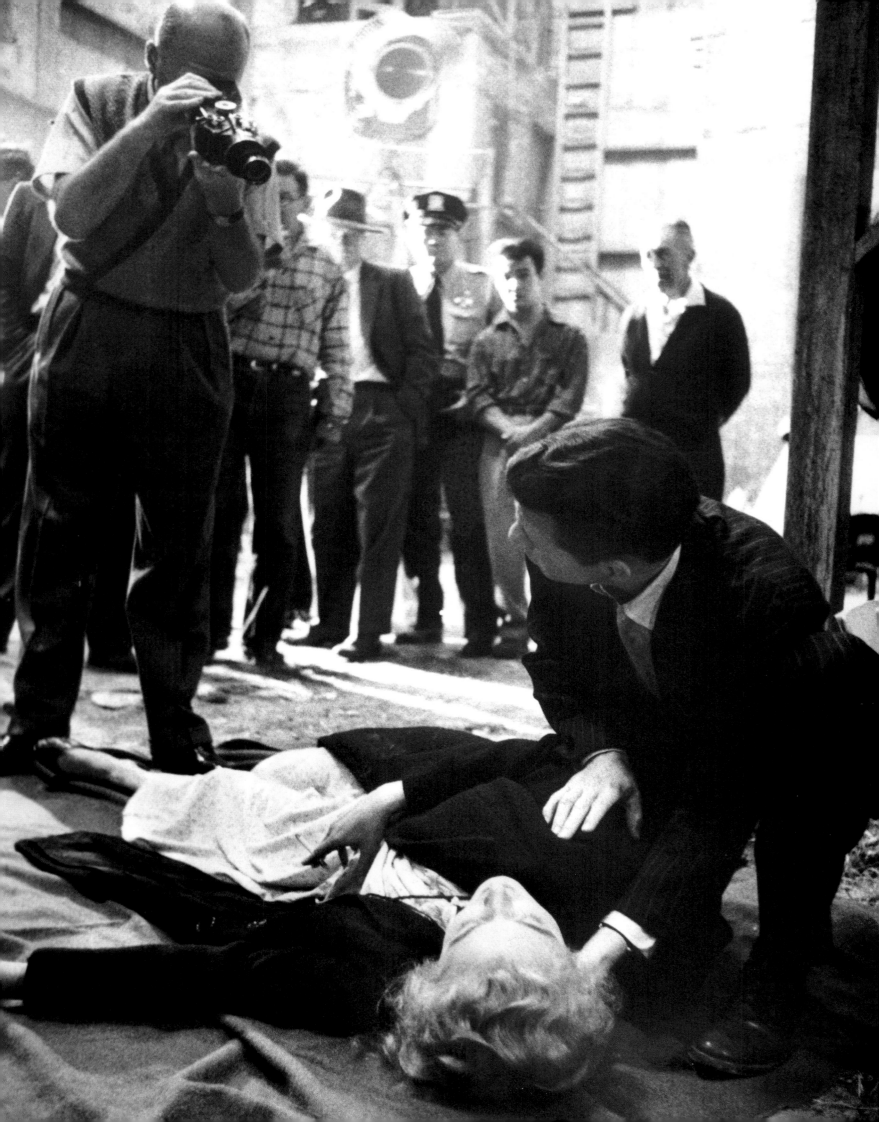

← ← Preminger sets up the poker sequence while Sinatra studies his script.

↓ The poker sequence, in which Frankie's creepy drug dealer Louie demands Frankie cheats to pay him for the drugs. (left to right) Robert Strauss, Darren McGavin and Sinatra.

↘ Sinatra with Joe McTurk.

→ → Of course the inevitable happens: Williams (George Matthews) catches Frankie cheating and beats him senseless.

Not all of the scenes were hard on Frank. Kim Novak's name springs to mind... Frank and Kim's relationship seemed somewhat distant in the beginning, but one could see the looks developing as the weeks went on. Later in the press we read the romance had caught fire.

At the time, though, there were just hints around the edges. I had thought Otto and Kim were having a flutter, but that was just a feeling, without any real knowledge of what was going on.

↓ Starting rehearsals for the drug withdrawal sequence, Preminger, Frank and Kim rehearse together on the darkened set.

↓ Kim starts the scene in which she pleads with Frankie to go through with the horrific cold-turkey withdrawal to free him of his heroin addiction.

→ Otto stops Kim in her tracks, demonstrating how she should put more fire and determination in her acting. Easy for Otto, hard for Kim.

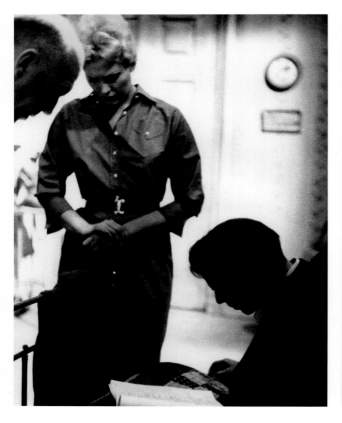

Sinatra's eye, dilated for a scene in the film. Molly holds up
a match to see if he is still taking drugs.

Sinatra begins rehearsals for the sequence in which Frankie valiantly tries to rid himself of the drugs with Molly's help. Preminger watches with the crew to see where they will place the camera.

Molly has locked Frankie in her room during his withdrawal. He will try anything to get out, as the pain is so great he thinks he is dying - he will tell her anything to get her to unlock the door. Finally, in his delirium, he breaks a chair and threatens to hit her with it. Molly holds her ground, and he backs down, falling exhausted to the floor.

Frankie eats sugar to fight off the effects of the drug withdrawal.

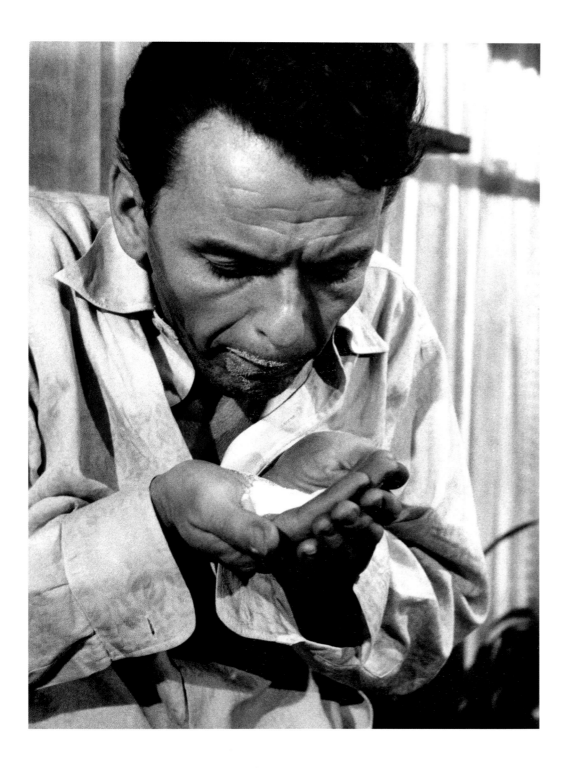

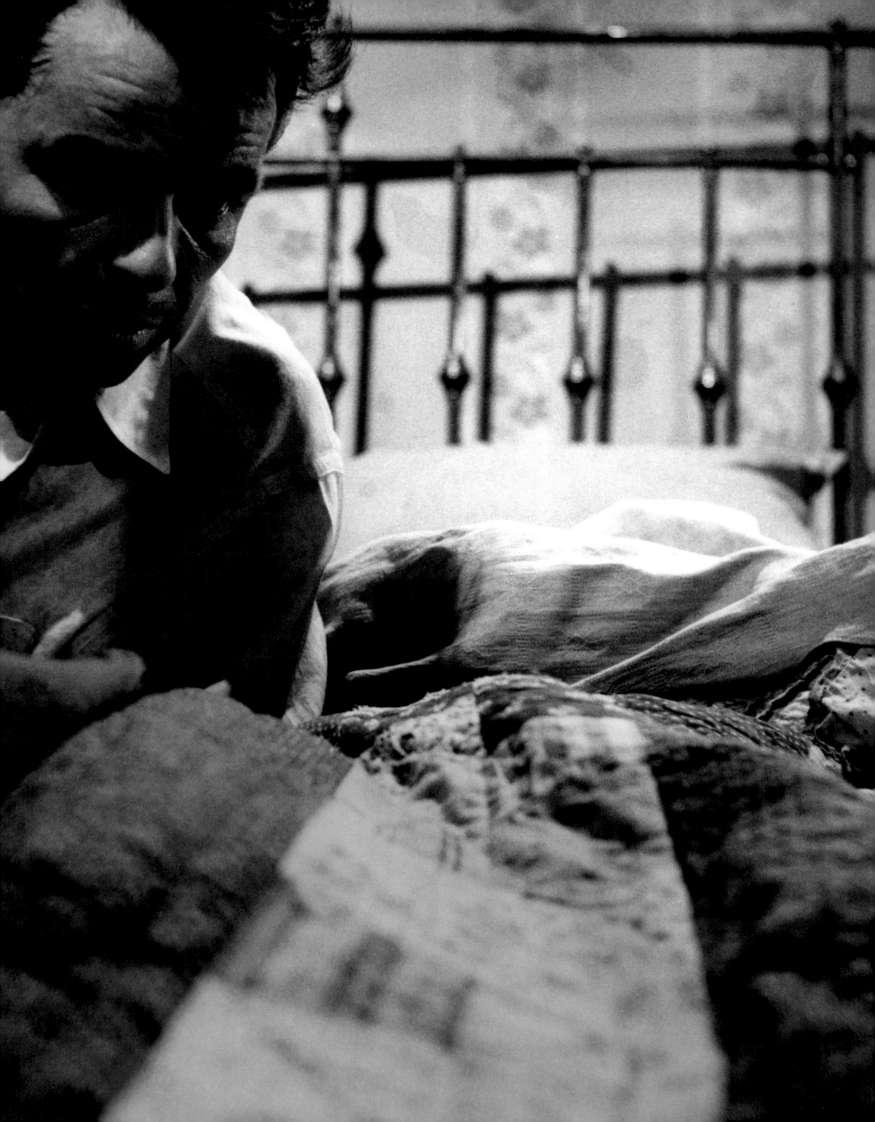

Sinatra went through this harrowing withdrawal sequence only once. Even though Preminger called for another take. Frank looked up at the camera operator, and when he nodded that he had gotten it, Frank left the set.

I've heard that Frank did this on some recording sessions. When he felt he had done what he had set out to do, that was it. On the other hand, I've heard he would record something over and over if he didn't feel it was perfect.

For me to photograph this scene was a real challenge, as there were no real rehearsals, and the motion picture camera was where the action was. In frustration, I climbed up into the lights above, and with long lenses was able to document this sequence.

Sinatra won an Academy Award nomination for his role as Frankie Machine. If there was any question in anyone's mind as to whether Frank was an actor or not, this resolved that once and for all.

Here are Frank's two usual expressions in this film: tense with total concentration for the coming scene, and happy relief when it was over. Sometimes it seemed like a kid getting out of school.

I found that not talking to Sinatra when we were working on set seemed to make me more invisible to him, giving me a rare opportunity to document the making of a film without being a distraction.

Jerry Lewis comes to visit and cracks Sinatra up. It was a welcome laugh on the set of such a downbeat film.

→ A young Robert Wagner visits from the filming of The Mountain at Paramount Studios, which was just next door to RKO. Jerry Lewis and the famous fighter Rocky Marciano also came to say hello and watch Frank perform.

Visitors were not common on this film, as Frank didn't seem to want any distractions. I didn't see any of the columnists who would normally cover a production. I think by this time many of them were giving Frank a wide berth.

The Man with the Golden Arm

Recording Session 1955

After the filming was completed, there was the film score to record. I went over the Hollywood studio and found a totally different Sinatra from the one I had worked with for the last five weeks, smiling and relaxed. I mentioned this amazing change to him. He looked at me as if I were his retarded son, and said, "Bobby, this is what I do!" And so it was.

↓ Sinatra stops the orchestra and checks the score while the studio
musicians wait, probably never having seen an artist take over
from a conductor before.

↓ Sinatra sets the tempo, while Elmer Bernstein, seemingly unfazed,
↓ continues with the rehearsal.

The composer of the Academy Award-winning film
score, Elmer Bernstein, was there directing the
orchestra. As Frank listened he just stepped in and
started directing the orchestra himself... softer here,
a change of tempo there... he knew what he was
doing, but there were no apologies to Elmer. Frank
was boss.

The rehearsals continued, and I was amused when
Otto Preminger came out of the booth where he had
been watching, to offer Frank some advice on the
score. Frank just looked at him... no way. He was the
director now!

After the session, I persuaded Frank to let me take some color portraits in the little park next to the recording studio.

He was still in a happy and relaxed mood, as the session had gone well. He posed for a few minutes, gave me a wink and then was gone.

I stood watching as he disappeared down the street. I don't know how to describe the feeling I had, other than that I had just been part of something very special.

University High School
1955

Frank agreed to give a concert for the student body of his daughter Nancy's high school, and she was to duet with him on a couple of songs. When I met them, Nancy had a bad case of stage fright.

It was interesting to see Frank fussing over her, playing the doting father and reassuring her that everything would be fine when the moment came.

Daughters can twist their fathers around their little fingers, and Frank was no exception to the rule.

↓ Frank and Nancy wait backstage for their moment together. Frank's expression, which shows the quiet gentle pleasure of performing with his daughter, was a side of Frank I had never seen. Frank's long-time accompanist Bill Miller is on the left.

Frank's singing was as smooth as melted chocolate in this performance, which showcased all his romantic classics. Through the side of the curtains, I could see the concentration of the students. This was a treat they could not have dreamed would happen.

Then it was Nancy's turn to join her father, and she was just terrific. Together they brought the house down, and you could see on Frank's face how proud he was of her.

Can
Can
1959

Frank had made about a dozen films before our
paths crossed again in 1959, on the film version
of the Broadway show *Can Can*. I used to see him
when he was doing *High Society* at MGM, as I was
on the adjoining stage, working on *Green Mansions*
with Audrey Hepburn. This is the first time we had
worked together since the Preminger film.

It was just after my wedding when 20th Century
Fox called, interrupting my honeymoon, asking me
to begin work on two of their films.

The first evening was the pre-recording session
with Frank and Maurice Chevalier. Nelson Riddle
had rehearsed the studio orchestra, and everyone
was waiting for Frank to appear.

He seemed in a happy mood when he arrived,
but when he saw the music score that had been
prepared, he said he wasn't doing it. This was a
major problem for the studio, as their orchestra
was waiting. Even the explanations of his trusted
friends Nelson Riddle and Saul Chaplin could not
change his mind.

It was all fun and games as Frank settled in for the pre-recording session at 20th Century Fox Studios. From left to right are musical director Saul Chaplin, producer Jack Cummings and Maurice Chevalier. Frank had just been handed the music they had prepared for the session, and that's when the evening began to fall apart.

The mood changes and Frank doesn't like what he sees. Maurice Chevalier scratches his head, as he doesn't know what the problem is. Frank waves his hat for the musical arranger Nelson Riddle to come over.

Jack Cummings has a serious talk with Frank, who won't budge. Cummings has an entire orchestra waiting, and any delays are very costly.

← Nelson Riddle arrives, standing with hands on his hips. He's been through this before, but he doesn't seem to be able to change Frank's mind. Maurice Chevalier, in the background, puts his glasses on and tries to figure out what to do.

↓ Nelson Riddle talks with Saul Chaplin about a possible change, as Frank waits. Chevalier just sits it out, as he has no say in any of this.

↓ Everyone waits for Frank. All of the suggestions seem to have gone nowhere.

↓ Now Frank is on his feet. Somehow he feels wronged, or maybe there was some misunderstanding. Nelson Riddle and Saul Chaplin listen to the complaint. People from every department have gathered round.

Bobby Tucker, the vocal supervisor, is in a white shirt and tie at centre right. Chevalier just waits it out, while Cummings, with his hands on his hips at the right, quietly fumes.

↓ Someone from the head office is brought down to see if they can resolve the conflict.

↓ The studio orchestra sits and waits, while a frustrated and now silent Nelson Riddle waits to see when he can start to do his job.

↓ Saul Chaplin comes up with a possible solution, but first he must clear it with vocal supervisor Bobby Tucker, in a white shirt, and choreographer Hermes Pan, in a black shirt on the right. Any change in the music requires a change in the chorus and the choreography. With that cleared, he shows Sinatra where the changes are. Nelson Riddle is finally able to rehearse the revised score with the orchestra.

→ Sinatra now details to patient Maurice Chevalier how the changes will affect the song they are about to record.

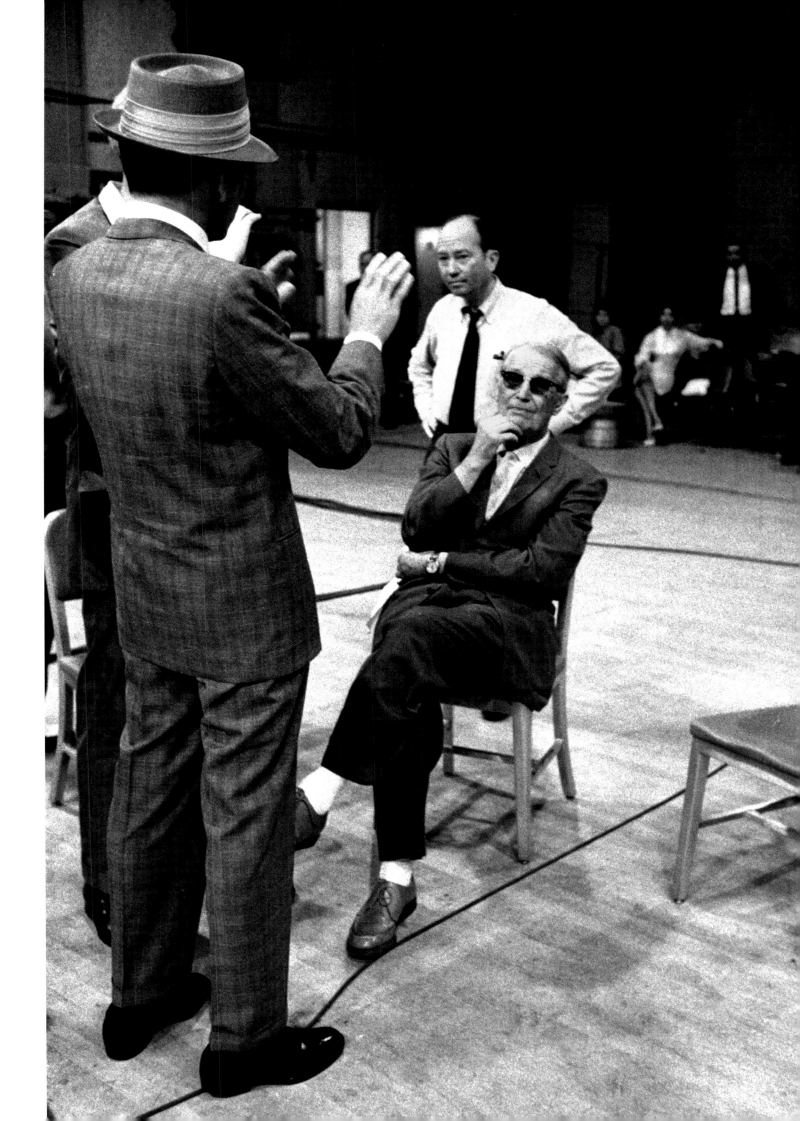

When the recording session was finally over, everyone concerned left with relief. I came home with some great images that document how film producers get gray hair and ulcers very quickly.

In the film, Sinatra has his eye on one of the can-can dancers in his favorite watering hole. As a thank-you for anticipated favours, he brings a very fancy garter for Shirley MacLaine. Maurice Chevalier smiles with knowing approval.

The evening of the can-can is interrupted by a police raid. Sinatra and Chevalier pretend to be waiters to avoid arrest. MacLaine, hiding under the table, bites Frank's leg because he hasn't interceded for her girls.

→ → Rehearsals, when they were with Frank and Shirley, were always happy ones. Shirley became the adopted mascot of Frank's famous Rat Pack. They interacted with a lot of shared enthusiasm.

← ← Frank, and musical director and associate producer Saul Chaplin, have a heart to heart behind the set. One of Chaplin's jobs was trying to keep Frank sweet during production.

↓ Rehearsals for the Cole Porter song "Let's Do It" ended with Frank unexpectedly landing on the floor. The two of them unquestionably enjoyed each other's company during the filming.

→ → Frank was having fun on set with Shirley MacLaine, but he seemed to have other things in mind for Juliet Prowse. Frank had only to give the ladies his little-boy-lost look, and they all seemed to melt into his arms.

The old groaner Bing Crosby came visiting on the Can Can set. At one time, the press had invented a feud between them. Bing had been the biggest-selling recording artist until Frank came on the scene. He once was quoted as saying:

"A voice like Frank Sinatra's comes once in a lifetime, but why did it have to be in my lifetime?" But they seemed to be great pals, and were wonderful together in High Society.

Frank seemed to be up one minute and down the next. Sometimes he looked so wistful that one felt he wished he were somewhere else, and then he would be entertaining visitors like Bob Wagner and Natalie Wood and having a great time. Natalie was another of the young ladies that the columnists linked romantically with Frank at one time or another.

Night shooting on the 20th Century Fox lot: we were waiting for production to begin. Frank didn't like to be kept waiting, and he would give Jack Cummings hell for calling him out when the camera man was still lighting the set.

Back in the recording studio, where this time the orchestra had been pre-recorded - Frank had only to sing along. The tension was gone, the film was basically over, and Frank was in a clowning mood with Shirley MacLaine, who was always a great audience.

What surprised me was listening to Frank sing when only he could hear the music. It didn't sound right somehow, until I heard the combined tracks played back. It was so curious that at one point I thought he could be singing off key.

I think anyone who wants to learn something from the way Frank sang should separate the tracks. He seemed to be singing against the music at times, like improvising on an instrument: it was amazing.

Ocean's 11
1960

I went to Las Vegas to cover a little of the filming on *Ocean's 11*, but it was soon clear the real story was the marathon lifestyle that Frank and his Rat Pack were living.

While I was there, he was filming all day, and at the same time doing a little cameo on the George Sidney film *Pepe*, with the great Mexican comic Cantinflas.

Then they all did The Sands' supper show, billed as "The Summit Meeting". They were drinking, gambling and seeing the ladies, and thinking up stunts to pull on each other for the following night's show… their stamina was incredible.

I marvel at it to this day. I feel I was fortunate as I was only needed there for a week!

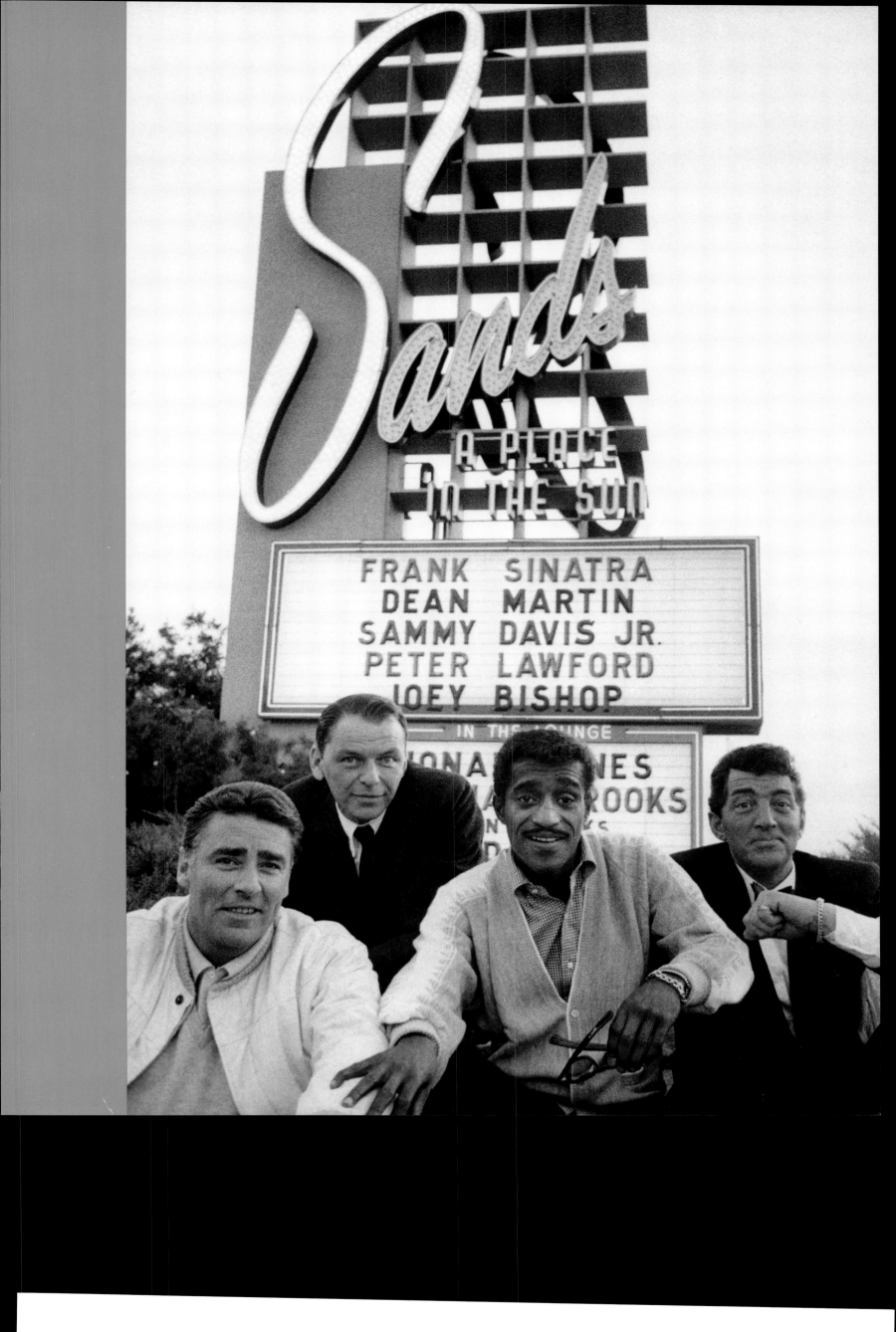

FRANK SINATRA
DEAN MARTIN
SAMMY DAVIS JR.
PETER LAWFORD
JOEY BISHOP

Frank talks to the troops after seeing the latest rushes of
the film. Sammy Davis Jr is on the right, with Patrice Wymore
behind Frank.

↓ Frank listens to director Louis Milestone before the filming begins. Comedian Buddy Lester plays the part of a porter in the centre.

↓ A scene from Ocean's 11: Frank with Richard Conte.

← ← Frank and Jack Entratter, the director of The Sands, have a chat while the camera crew on Pepe set up for Frank's cameo appearance.

Frank's habit of acting as though he owned
The Sands amazed me - the way he walked
around the place, or when he would go behind
the blackjack table and take the deck away from
the dealer... I always wondered how he could
do that.

I discovered later that he actually did own part
of The Sands, and with Jack Entratter he had the
run of the place.

↓ I just followed this tireless man. When there was a break, and Frank wasn't filming, he would go backstage to rehearse his songs for the supper show. Whenever he came in, the dancers had to stop their rehearsal, as he was the boss. He would lock in the changes he had in mind, and then he was off.

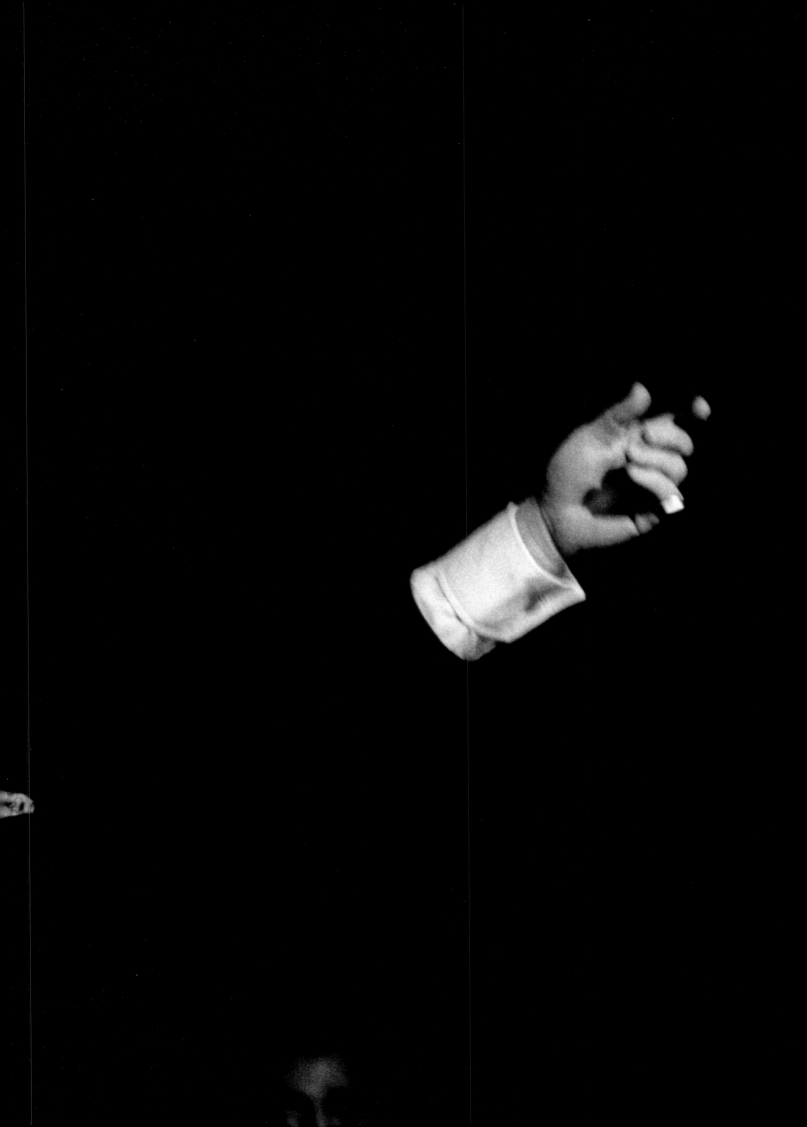

The "Summit Meeting" of the Rat Pack: Dean Martin, Sammy Davis Jr, Peter Lawford, Sinatra, Buddy Lester and Joey Bishop. Here Buddy Lester breaks into the melody with one of his famous jokes and cracks everyone up. One night, Lester walked on stage in his shorts while Frank was singing. Another night, right in the middle of Sammy's song, they hit him in the face with a cream cake.

And then there was the "Summit Meeting" when Frank came alive in front of the live audience. The idea during each night's performance was to crack each other up, and no one was sacred. The supper crowd seemed to love these hi-jinks. I was never sure who was having more fun: the audience or the cast on stage.

↓ Frank poses backstage for one of the Las Vegas Indians. The drum is Frank's gag for the night, as he owned Puccini's. He would wear the drum on stage when Dean Martin was trying to sing. Dean also had his own restaurant, Dino's, at the time.

ON ST
OR IN

EAT AT PUCCINI

→ As Frank went by with the drum, everyone saluted. Then, when
Frank tried to sing, Dean slid past him into an imaginary home
plate. Buddy Lester, in a baseball umpire's hat, declared him safe.
And they partied on.

↓ Sitting on the ledge are Peter, Frank and Frank's banker Al Hart;
  lying down is Sammy Davis.

To recharge their energy after the evening show,
some of them would retire to The Sands' steam room
and sweat it out - and seem to be ready to go again.

Frank, ever restless, had a need to be doing something. I never saw him sitting alone. He filled his time with endless activities.

Some of the games he played were wildly exciting, a lifestyle that many envied. Others found his pursuits rather frantic. I wonder if there was ever time for a moment of quiet within.

Judy Garland's TV Show
1962

I had just photographed what was to be Judy Garland's last film, *I Could Go On Singing*, and Judy had serious emotional problems.

When Dean and Frank were to be guests on Judy's NBC-TV show, I was asked to photograph it. I didn't know quite what to expect after the London film.

The boys loved Judy, and both of them were wonderful with her. They went out of their way to keep her laughing all the time. It was great to see her happy again and in such rare form.

As Mort Lindsay conducts the NBC orchestra, Dean, Judy and
Frank pre-record the songs for the evening's performance.

→ "It's a quarter to three, and there ain't no one here except you and me," Martin and Sinatra sing, and the legend continues.

The show was spontaneous, funny and full of the energy associated with people of great talent. When Judy sang, at times you could feel the hairs on the back of your neck rise... she was unique, as were Frank and Dean. We're not likely to see the likes of them ever again.

Marriage on the Rocks
1965

The last time I worked with Frank was in this slight little flick at Warner Brothers. It was with Dean Martin, Deborah Kerr and Frank's daughter Nancy. I think it was made mostly to prop up Frank's now-ailing image.

I was working on another film on the Warner lot. There was nothing much in this one for the magazines, except, of course, for the wonderful luck of Frank unknowingly posing under this sign as he waited for filming to commence.

It had been ten years since I photographed Frank with his daughter. Nancy, though no longer a school-girl, is obviously still Frank's little girl. He was there to cheer her up and listen to her problems as they walk off the Warner Brothers set together.

↓ Frank and Nancy with Prince Mike Romanoff, the famous Hollywood restauranteur, who was visiting the set. Everyone knew he wasn't a prince, but he was a celebrated figure in the Hollywood scene for years, and a good friend of Frank's.

↓ Frank meets one of the extras on the Mexican set.

→ Waiting was one of Frank's least favourite things to do. Here he waits for the assistant to call to say the camera was ready.

→ Martin cracks Sinatra up during a rehearsal as he tries to squeeze
through the chained door - which definitely wasn't in the script.

In 1965, Warner Brothers had assigned me to photograph *Who's Afraid of Virginia Woolf?* with then-reigning box office stars Elizabeth Taylor and Richard Burton.

I found it interesting to see that, after photographing all the visitors who paid court to Frank when he was filming, he now came to visit the Burtons. Times change.

It was the last time I would ever see Frank, as my assignments often took me away from Hollywood for extended periods. But Frank's lustre never dimmed. He made film after film, and the great recordings he made are being played to this day.

He was bigger than life: he had something special; the rare talent that meant when he sang, it was difficult, if not impossible, to ignore that ol' black magic in his voice.

His is the benchmark to which young singers aspire, and he increased our appreciation of the popular song like no other.

Thank you, Francis Albert Sinatra!

Photography
Bob Willoughby

Art Direction and Book Design
OPX, London

Reprographics
AJD Colour Ltd

Print
Oriental Press

First published in Great Britain in 2002
by Vision On Publishing Ltd
112-116 Old Street
London EC1V 9BG
T +44 (0)20 7336 0766
F +44 (0)20 7336 0966
www.vobooks.com
info@visiononpublishing.com

All photography © Bob Willoughby
All text © Bob Willoughby

Book design © OPX Design

The right of Bob Willoughby to be identified as
the author of his work has been asserted by him in
accordance with the Copyright, Designs and
Patents Act of 1988.

ISBN 1 903399 65 3 (softback)
ISBN 1 903399 72 6 (hardback)

Printed in Dubai